JIMMIE JOHNSON

KENNY ABDO

Fly!
An Imprint of Abdo Zoom
abdobooks.com

abdobooks.com

Published by Abdo Zoom, a division of ABDO, P.O. Box 398166, Minneapolis, Minnesota 55439. Copyright © 2022 by Abdo Consulting Group, Inc. International copyrights reserved in all countries. No part of this book may be reproduced in any form without written permission from the publisher. Fly!™ is a trademark and logo of Abdo Zoom.

Printed in the United States of America, North Mankato, Minnesota.
102021
012022

THIS BOOK CONTAINS
RECYCLED MATERIALS

Photo Credits: Alamy, AP Images, Getty Images, iStock, Shutterstock
Production Contributors: Kenny Abdo, Jennie Forsberg, Grace Hansen
Design Contributors: Candice Keimig, Neil Klinepier

Library of Congress Control Number: 2021940213

Publisher's Cataloging-in-Publication Data

Names: Abdo, Kenny, author.
Title: Jimmie Johnson / by Kenny Abdo
Description: Minneapolis, Minnesota : Abdo Zoom, 2022 | Series: NASCAR biographies |
    Includes online resources and index.
Identifiers: ISBN 9781098226824 (lib. bdg.) | ISBN 9781644946855 (pbk.) |
    ISBN 9781098227661 (ebook) | ISBN 9781098228088 (Read-to-Me ebook)
Subjects: LCSH: Johnson, Jimmie, 1975---Juvenile literature. | Automobile racing
    drivers--Biography--Juvenile literature. | Stock car drivers--Biography--Juvenile
    literature. | NASCAR (Association)--Juvenile literature. | Stock car racing--Juvenile
    literature.
Classification: DDC 796.72092--dc23

TABLE OF CONTENTS

Jimmie Johnson 4

Early Years 8

The Big Time 12

Legacy 18

Glossary 22

Online Resources 23

Index 24

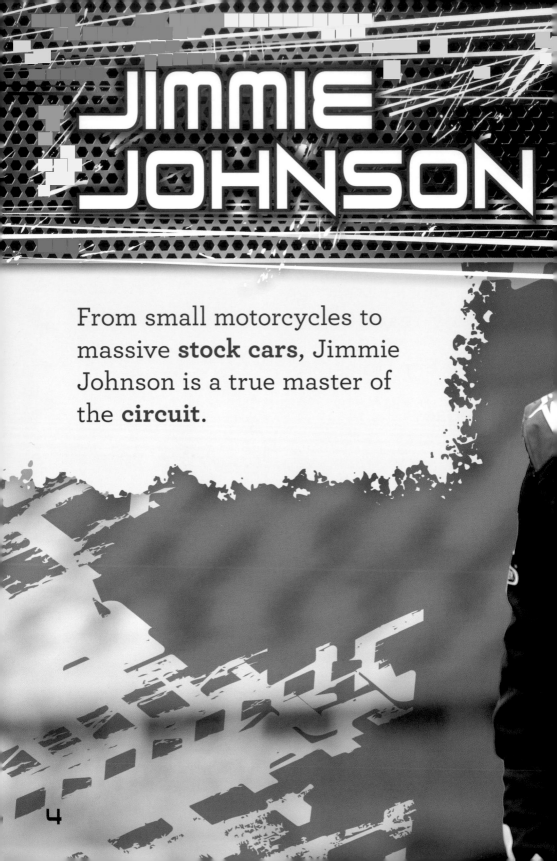

JIMMIE JOHNSON

From small motorcycles to massive **stock cars**, Jimmie Johnson is a true master of the **circuit**.

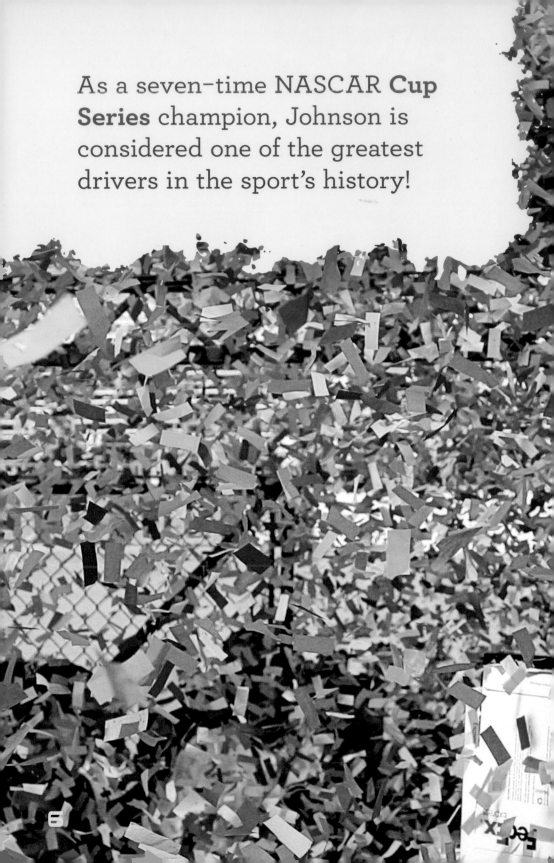

As a seven-time NASCAR **Cup Series** champion, Johnson is considered one of the greatest drivers in the sport's history!

EARLY
YEARS

Jimmie Johnson was born in El Cajon, California, in 1975.

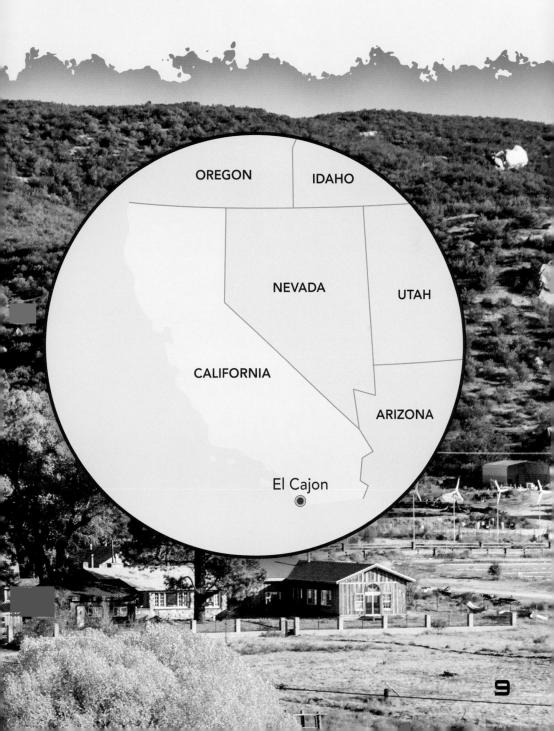

By the age of five, Johnson was racing small motorcycles. He won his first **championship** at just eight years old!

Johnson shifted gears and began **off-road** racing in his late teens. By 1998, he had won six **championships** and the **Rookie** of the Year award. Johnson was ready for the big leagues!

THE BIG TIME

Johnson made his first appearance
in the NASCAR Winston **Cup Series**
in 2001. The next year, he began his
rookie season in the Cup Series. He
won three races, ending the season in
fifth place.

Johnson won his first **Cup Series championship** in 2006. He scored five victories, including the **Daytona 500**!

Johnson won seven races in 2009, earning his fourth title. He became the first NASCAR driver to be named Male Athlete of the Year by the Associated Press!

Johnson won a seventh career NASCAR title in 2016. That tied him with Dale Earnhardt Sr. for the most **championships** for a driver in **Cup Series** history!

In 2019, Johnson announced the next season would be his last. Even though the 2020 season was hugely interrupted by COVID-19, he finished his career with ten top-ten finishes!

LEGACY

Johnson has won the impressive ESPY award for Best Driver in both 2008 and 2009. He won the Martini & Rossi Driver of the Year award an incredible five times!

19

The Jimmie Johnson Foundation was launched in 2006 by Johnson and his wife, Chandra. The **charity** supports and promotes health, education, and disaster relief.

Johnson is a NASCAR legend who started small and ended his career with a mighty engine roar.

GLOSSARY

championship – a game held to find a first-place winner.

charity – an organization set up to provide help and raise money for those in need.

circuit – another name for a track that races are held on.

Cup Series – the top racing series of NASCAR where 16 drivers compete for the championship. The first nine races are three rounds, with four participants cut after each.

Daytona 500 – the most famous stock car race in the world and one of the races in the Spring Cup Series.

off-road – riding a vehicle on difficult roads or tracks, like sand, mud or gravel.

rookie – a first-year player in a professional sport.

series – a set of events in order.

stock car – a normal car that has been customized for racing.

ONLINE RESOURCES

Booklinks
NONFICTION NETWORK
FREE! ONLINE NONFICTION RESOURCES

To learn more about Jimmie Johnson, please visit abdobooklinks.com or scan this QR code. These links are routinely monitored and updated to provide the most current information available.

INDEX

California 9

Coronavirus disease 17

Daytona 500 14

Earnhardt Sr., Dale 16

ESPY Awards 18

Jimmie Johnson Foundation, The 20

Johnson, Chandra 20

Martini & Rossi Awards 18

races 10, 11, 13, 14, 15, 16

retirement 17